To:

From:

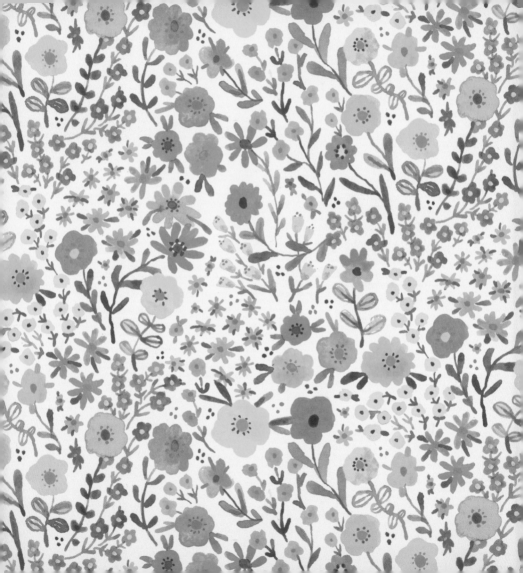

I Wish for You

Lance Wubbels and Shannon Snow

TEN PEAKS PRESS®
EUGENE, OR

Cover and interior design by Dugan Design Group

For bulk or special sales, please call 1 800-547-8979.
Email: Customerservice@hhpbooks.com

 This logo is a trademark of the Hawkins Children's LLC. Harvest House
Publishers, Inc., is the exclusive licensee of this trademark.

I Wish for You

Text copyright © 2022 by Lance Wubbels

Artwork © 2022 by Shannon Snow, courtesy of Jewel Branding & Licensing, Inc.

Published by Ten Peaks Press, an imprint of Harvest House Publishers
Eugene, Oregon 97408

ISBN 978-0-7369-8628-1 (hardcover)

Printed in China

22 23 24 25 26 27 28 29 30 / LP / 10 9 8 7 6 5 4 3 2 1

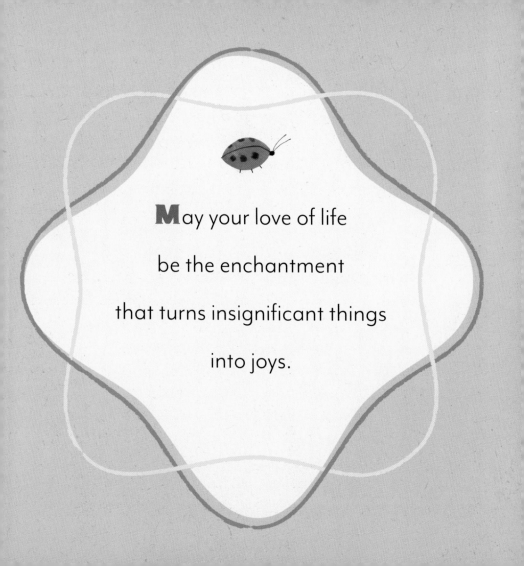

May your love of life

be the enchantment

that turns insignificant things

into joys.

I wish for you

dreams so big

that you have to grow into them.

I hope you will always

feel fearlessly free

to be you.

May you always see

that happiness is found

in what you have,

not in striving

for what you don't have.

May your greatest joys

not be in toys,

may your best things not be things,

and may your riches always be in the

treasury of your heart.

I hope your thoughts

always keep you

in good company.

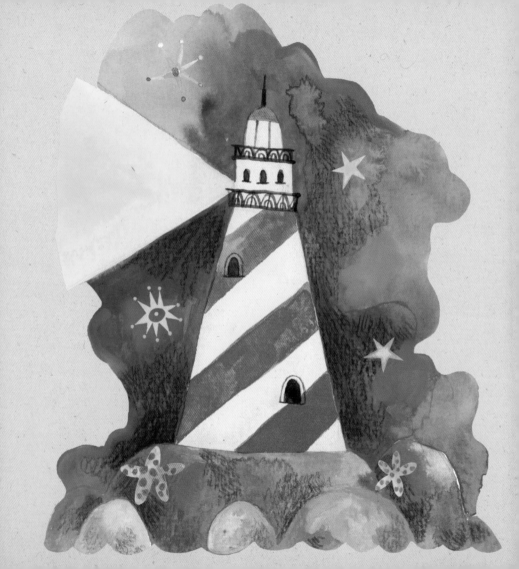

When shadows fall

and the path you walk grows dark,

may the smile of God light your way.

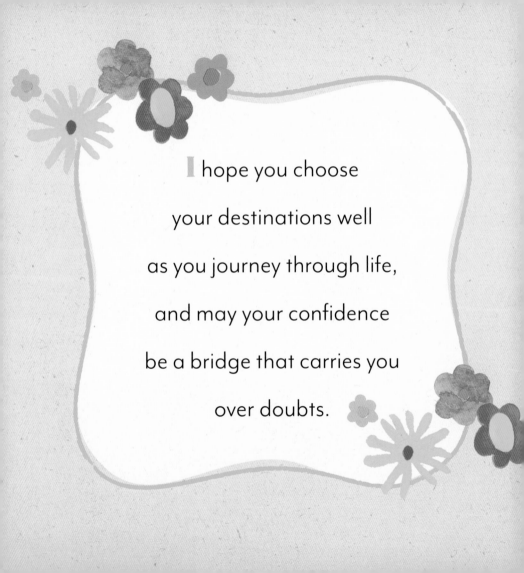

I hope you choose

your destinations well

as you journey through life,

and may your confidence

be a bridge that carries you

over doubts.

I wish for you

the courage of conviction,

the strength to persevere,

and the hope that survives

all trials.

I hope you tend well

the garden of your soul.

When you know you're right,

I hope you never change or compromise

just because you're outnumbered.

May you see sunshine

where others see shadows

and opportunities

where others see obstacles.

I hope you will rely on God's love

to help you turn large problems into little ones

and little ones into nothing at all.

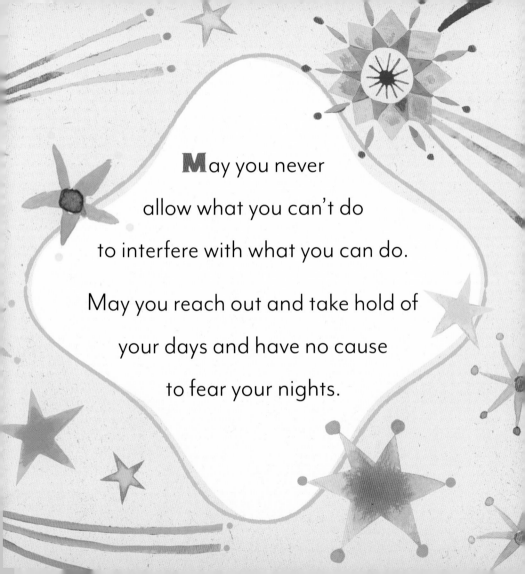

May you never

allow what you can't do

to interfere with what you can do.

May you reach out and take hold of

your days and have no cause

to fear your nights.

When your soul is weary and troubled,

I hope you remember

"The Lord is my shepherd."

He'll lead you beside quiet waters.

May you have

the fortitude and faith

to hang on to what's important

when others have let go.

May your failures and mistakes

become steps of learning

on your path to better tomorrows.

I hope you will live

with the sense of wonder

and openness

and trust

and forgiveness

of a child.

I wish that you

never have a day without

laughing or loving,

giving or forgiving.

May you take time

to quiet your soul,

silence the noise in your head and heart,

and remind yourself of what

you really want out of life.

I hope you will dare

to follow the stepping-stones

from the known to the unknown,

and to do the undoable.

May you realize that

all great achievements take time.

And when you achieve great things,

I hope you stay humble in heart.

I wish for you

the inner clarity of light

that never allows

a small worry

to cast a big shadow.

May you always find

the sparkle that's hidden

in the dreariest of days.

When you hug,

I hope you hug tight.

When you talk,

I hope you talk with your eyes.

When you listen,

I hope you listen with your heart.

May you learn to sail in all winds

and across the seas of change.

When your world feels like it's falling apart,

I hope your friends, family, and faith

are the bonds that hold it together.

May you believe that God

can breathe new life into your dreams

and fill your days with second chances.

I wish for you

freedom from regrets

and from bitterness

and from trying to

settle scores.

I hope you take time

to shut your eyes

and look beyond

what you can see.

May your life be measured

not by the number of times

your heart beats

but by the number of moments

that capture your heart.

May you never have

too much of a good thing

or too little of what you need.

I hope that you truly live life now

and not wait

until,

until,

until...

I hope you can always

forget the things

that matter least

and remember the things

that are close to God's heart.

When the stormy winds of life

threaten to knock you down,

may you have the courage

to spread your wings and fly!

I hope you will

do what you love,

find work that makes you happy,

and live life with gusto.

I wish that you will

remain young at heart

for as long as you live.

I hope you will

always look up...

higher and higher...

and see life's endless possibilities.

May you love abundantly,

live abundantly,

and leave a legacy

rich with integrity.

I hope you realize your life

is truly your life...

it belongs to you.

It is your story

to write with love.

Day by day, line by line,

write it well.

Lance Wubbels is the author of several award-winning books, including *To a Child Love Is Spelled T-I-M-E*, *One Small Miracle*, and *In His Presence*. He also wrote many bestselling gift books for Hallmark. With more than 40 years of experience in the publishing industry, Lance has been blessed to work with such notables as T.D. Jakes, Max Lucado, and many more. He and his wife make their home in Minnesota.

Shannon Snow is an illustrator and designer whose vibrant and colorful creations have appeared on several popular products in the home, gift, and apparel categories. Shannon and her husband live in Georgia with their two young children.

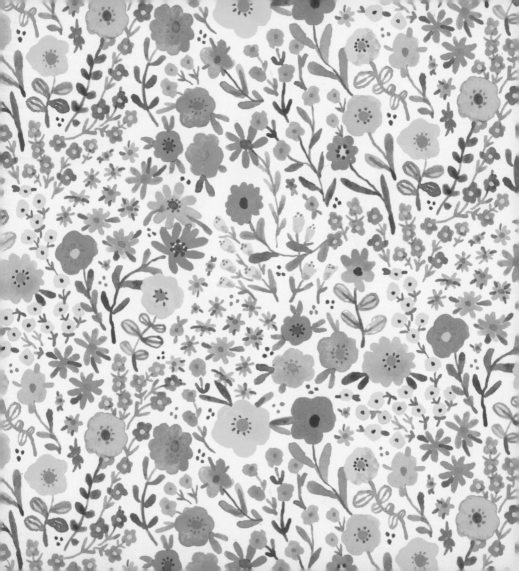